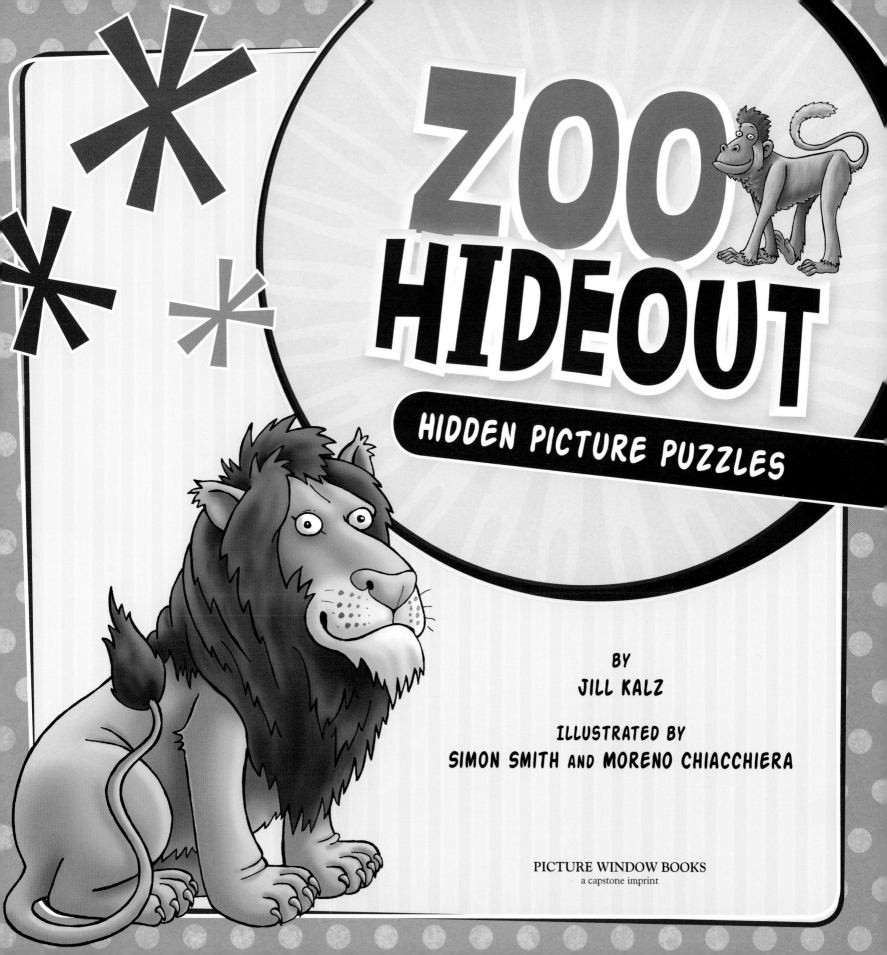

ZOO HIDEOUT

HIDDEN PICTURE PUZZLES

BY
JILL KALZ

ILLUSTRATED BY
SIMON SMITH AND MORENO CHIACCHIERA

PICTURE WINDOW BOOKS
a capstone imprint

DESIGNER: LORI BYE
ART DIRECTOR: NATHAN GASSMAN
PRODUCTION SPECIALIST: DANIELLE CEMINSKY
THE ILLUSTRATIONS IN THIS BOOK WERE CREATED DIGITALLY.

PICTURE WINDOW BOOKS
1710 ROE CREST DRIVE
NORTH MANKATO, MN 56003
WWW.CAPSTONEPUB.COM

Library of Congress Cataloging-in-Publication Data
Kalz, Jill.
 Zoo hideout : hidden picture puzzles / by Jill Kalz ; illustrated
by Simon Smith and Moreno Chiacchiera.
    p. cm.
 Summary: "Illustrated scenes related to the zoo invite readers
to find a list of objects hidden within them"—Provided by
publisher.
 ISBN 978-1-4048-7497-8 (library binding)
 ISBN 978-1-4048-7730-6 (paperback)
 ISBN 978-1-40487-994-2 (ebook PDF)
 1. Picture puzzles—Juvenile literature. I. Smith,
Simon, ill. II. Chiacchiera, Moreno, ill. III. Title.
 GV1507.P47K35 2013
 793.73—dc23   2012007186

Printed in the United States of America
in Stevens Point, Wisconsin.
032012   006678WZF12

DIRECTIONS:

Look at the pictures and find the items on the lists. Not too tough, right? Not for a clever kid like you. But be warned: The first few puzzles are tricky. The next ones are even trickier. And the final puzzles are for the bravest seekers only. Good luck!

TABLE OF CONTENTS

Tickets, Please

- monkey
- broom
- tiger
- penguin
- banjo
- bicycle

Farmyard Charm

- lunchbox
- lion
- hamburger
- corn
- bucket
- goat

Oh My, Butterfly

- airplane
- kite
- balloon
- owl
- bee
- bat

Say "Ahh"

- toothbrush
- watch
- leash
- star
- envelope
- magnifying glass

Splish, Splash, Clap, and Laugh

- seal
- pelican
- turtle
- boat
- flippers
- shark

13

Nice and Icy

- arctic hare
- ice-cream cone
- snowshoes
- lemming
- winter boot
- thermometer
- star
- airplane
- arctic fox

In the Mood for Food

- skateboard
- chicken
- panda
- pineapple
- fish
- ice-cream cone
- clown
- giraffe
- chef's hat

17

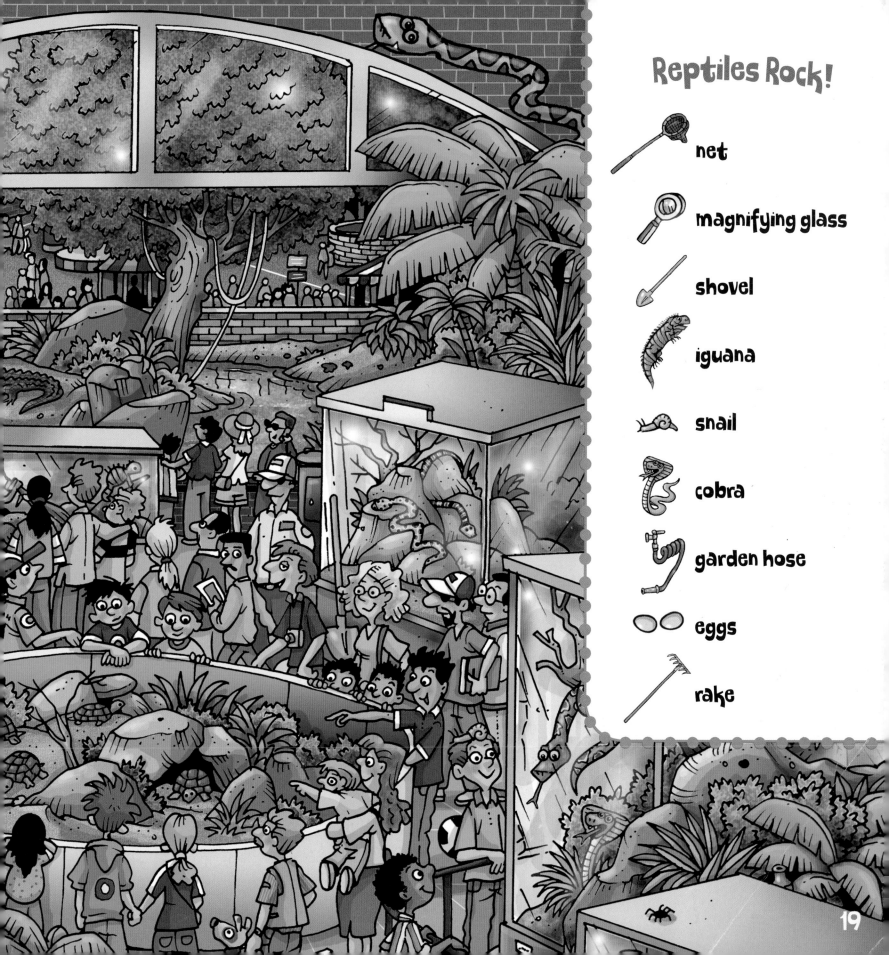

Reptiles Rock!

- net
- magnifying glass
- shovel
- iguana
- snail
- cobra
- garden hose
- eggs
- rake

Monkey Mischief

- telephone
- camera
- key
- sunglasses
- umbrella
- beads
- teddy bear
- dollar bill
- cotton candy

ZOO

20

A Tricky Tree

- snake
- parrot
- elephant
- lizard
- clover
- walrus
- zebra
- clock
- pretzel

Absolutely Africa

 mask

 Africa

 hippo

 African flag

 camel

 compass

 pyramid

 safari hat

 Sphinx

 sun

 drum

 African Hare

24

See the Deep Sea

 volleyball

 treasure chest

 hook

 ring

 pirate

 coin

 crown

 anchor

 eel

 boot

 flamingo

 marble

Winging It

 lobster

 cheetah

 fox

 snake

 salamander

 panther

 wolf

 octopus

 kangaroo

 fish

 mountain goat

 mouse

Good Buys

 flowers

 puzzle piece

 eagle

 map

 umbrella

 globe

 ruler

 turtle

 baseball

 racquet

 cherry

 duck

30

FOUND EVERYTHING?

Not quite! Flip back and see if you can find these sneaky items.

scissors

popsicle

saxophone

submarine

gloves

calendar

paintbrush in a can

seeing-eye dog

truck

fire hydrant

Internet Sites

FactHound offers a safe, fun way to find Internet sites related to this book. All of the sites on FactHound have been researched by our staff.

Here's all you do:

Visit *www.facthound.com*

Type in this code: 9781404874978

look for all the books in the series:

CHRISTMAS CHAOS

HALLOWEEN HIDE AND SEEK

SCHOOL SHAKE-UP

ZOO HIDEOUT